UNDERSTANDING RENAL DIET

Quick And Easy Mouthwatering Recipes. Stay Healthy With
Low Sodium And Low Potassium Recipes

JOY ELLEDGE

Table of Contents

INTRODUCTION

When renal function is impaired, a renal diet is deficient in sodium, phosphorus, and potassium, three minerals that the body cannot adequately metabolize and flush out (in excess levels).

A renal diet adheres to a few basic principles. The first is that it must be a well-balanced, organic, and long-term diet that is high in whole grains, vitamins, fibers, carbohydrates, omega-3 fats, and fluids. Proteins should be enough, but not too many.

The Renal Diet Cookbook is for people who have been diagnosed with chronic kidney disease (CKD) and want to eat a balanced diet. The book contains basic, step-by-step, and easy-to-follow recipes, as well as for instructions for kidney patients. This guide was created to assist those with CKD in regaining lost weight and enjoying their favorite foods. The terms kidney function and renal function are used to describe how well the kidneys work. A pair of kidneys is born with every healthy person. As a result, when one of the kidneys stopped working, it went unnoticed because the other kidney was still working. However, if the kidney functions continue to deteriorate and hit a level as low as 25%, the situation becomes dangerous for the patients. People with only one working kidney need adequate external therapy and, in the worst-case scenario, a kidney transplant.

Renal Diet Cookbook aided you in learning more about your condition, making good decisions, and staying on track with the basics. We hope you've learned a lot more about your

Renal Diet as a result of this article. We recognize that the quality of our goods and services is just as critical as the quality of our knowledge at the Renal Diet Cookbook.

Potassium levels in salt substitutes can be high. Examine the affixing label. If you want to use salt derivatives, talk to your supplier. Before eating canned foods, run them through a screening machine. More advice on how to keep the levels of potassium in your blood at a healthy level. Choose new, ground-grown foods and avoid salt derivatives or subsidiaries, as well as potassium-based seasonings. Phosphorus can be present in a variety of foods. Patients with reduced kidney function can consult with a renal dietitian to keep track of their phosphorus levels.

It is a way of eating that protects your kidneys from more harm. It entails limiting a few ingredients and liquids to prevent such minerals from developing in your body. However, as the infection worsens and kidney failure worsens, you must become more vigilant about what you eat and drink.

Many foods fit well in the renal diet, and once you see how many options there are, it won't seem as restrictive or difficult to stick to. The trick is to concentrate on foods that are rich in nutrients, as these make it easier for the kidneys to absorb waste by reducing the amount of waste that the body has to discard. Long-term renal function depends on maintaining and enhancing balance.

BREAKFAST

1. Cheese Spaghetti Frittata

Preparation Time: 10 minutes

Cooking Time: 10 minutes

Servings: 6

Ingredients:

- 4 cups whole-wheat spaghetti, cooked
- 4 teaspoons olive oil
- 3 medium onions, chopped
- 4 large eggs
- 1/2 cup almond milk
- 1/3 cup Parmesan cheese, grated
- 2 tablespoons fresh parsley, chopped
- 2 tablespoons fresh basil, chopped
- 1/2 teaspoon black pepper
- 1 tomato, diced

Directions:

1. Set a suitable non-stick skillet over moderate heat and add in the olive oil.
2. Place the spaghetti in the skillet and cook by stirring for 2 minutes on moderate heat.
3. Whisk the eggs with almond milk, parsley, and black pepper in a bowl.
4. Pour this almond milky egg mixture over the spaghetti and top it all with basil, cheese, and tomato.

5. Cover the spaghetti frittata again with a lid and cook for approximately 8 minutes on low heat.
6. Slice and serve.

Nutrition: Calories 230,Total Fat 7.8g, Sodium 77mg, Dietary Fiber 5.6g, Sugars 4.5g, Protein 11.1g,

Calcium 88mg, Phosphorous 368 mg, Potassium 214mg,

2. Shrimp Bruschetta

Preparation Time: 15 minutes

Cooking Time: 10 minutes

Servings: 4

Ingredients:

- 13 oz. shrimps, peeled
- 1 tablespoon tomato sauce
- ½ teaspoon Splenda
- ¼ teaspoon garlic powder
- 1 teaspoon fresh parsley, chopped
- ½ teaspoon olive oil
- 1 teaspoon lemon juice
- 4 whole-grain bread slices
- 1 cup water, for cooking

Directions:

1. In the saucepan, pour water and bring it to boil.
2. Add shrimps and boil them over the high heat for 5 minutes.
3. After this, drain shrimps and chill them to the room temperature.
4. Mix up together shrimps with Splenda, garlic powder, tomato sauce, and fresh parsley.

5. Add lemon juice and stir gently.
6. Preheat the oven to 360f.
7. Coat the slice of bread with olive oil and bake for 3 minutes.
8. Then place the shrimp mixture on the bread. Bruschetta is cooked.

Nutrition: Calories 199, Fat 3.7, Fiber 2.1, Carbs 15.3,Protein 24.1 Calcium 79mg,

Phosphorous 316mg, Potassium 227mg Sodium: 121 mg

3. Strawberry Muesli

Preparation Time: 10 minutes

Cooking Time: 30 minutes

Servings: 4

Ingredients:

- 2 cups Greek yogurt
- 1 ½ cup strawberries, sliced
- 1 ½ cup Muesli
- 4 teaspoon maple syrup
- ¾ teaspoon ground cinnamon

Directions:

1. Put Greek yogurt in the food processor.
2. Add 1 cup of strawberries, maple syrup, and ground cinnamon.
3. Blend the ingredients until you get smooth mass.
4. Transfer the yogurt mass in the serving bowls.
5. Add Muesli and stir well.
6. Leave the meal for 30 minutes in the fridge.

7. After this, decorate it with remaining sliced strawberries.

Nutrition: Calories 149, Fat 2.6, Fiber 3.6,Carbs 21.6, Protein 12 Calcium 69mg, Phosphorous 216mg, Potassium 227mg Sodium: 151 mg

4. Yogurt Bulgur

Preparation Time: 10 minutes

Cooking Time: 15 minutes

Servings: 3

Ingredients:

- 1 cup bulgur
- 2 cups Greek yogurt
- 1 ½ cup water
- ½ teaspoon salt
- 1 teaspoon olive oil

Directions:

1. Pour olive oil in the saucepan and add bulgur.
2. Roast it over the medium heat for 2-3 minutes. Stir it from time to time.
3. After this, add salt and water.
4. Close the lid and cook bulgur for 15 minutes over the medium heat.
5. Then chill the cooked bulgur well and combine it with Greek yogurt. Stir it carefully.
6. Transfer the cooked meal into the serving plates. The yogurt bulgur tastes the best when it is cold.

Nutrition: Calories 274, Fat 4.9, Fiber 8.5, Carbs 40.8, Protein 19.2Calcium 39mg, Phosphorous 216mg, Potassium 237mg Sodium: 131 mg

LUNCH

5. Spaghetti with Pesto

Preparation Time: 10 minutes

Cooking Time: 10 minutes

Servings: 4

Ingredients:

- 8 ounces spaghetti (package pasta)
- 2 cups packed basil leaves
- 2 cups packed arugula leaves
- 1/3 cup walnut pieces
- 3 cloves of garlic
- ¼ cup extra-virgin olive oil
- Black pepper

Directions:

1. Cook pasta with boiling water. Drain.
2. Add the basil, garlic, olive oil, walnuts, pepper and arugula in a blender and mix until creamy.
3. Mix pesto mixture into pasta in a large bowl.
4. Serve and enjoy!

Nutrition: Calories 400 Fat 21 g Cholesterol 0 mg Carbohydrates 46 g Sugar 2 g Fiber 3 g Protein 11 g Sodium 6 mg Calcium 64 mg Phosphorus 113 mg Potassium 202 mg

6. Corn and Shrimp Quiche

Preparation Time: 15 minutes

Cooking Time: 50 minutes

Servings: 6

Ingredients:

- 1 cup small cooked shrimp
- 1½ cups frozen corn, thawed and drained
- 5 large eggs, beaten
- 1 cup unsweetened almond milk
- Pinch salt
- 1/8 teaspoon freshly ground black pepper

Directions:

1. Preheat the oven to 350°F. Spray a 9-inch pie pan with nonstick baking spray.
2. In the prepared pan, combine the shrimp and corn.
3. In a medium bowl, beat the eggs, almond milk, salt, and pepper. Gently pour into the pan.
4. Bake for 45 to 55 minutes or until the quiche is puffed, set to the touch, and light golden brown on top. Let stand for 10 minutes before cutting into wedges to serve.
5. Ingredient Tip: Shrimp are measured according to the number per pound. So bigger shrimp have a lower number per pound. For this recipe, small shrimp should be about 50 per pound. Medium shrimp are usually 36 to 40 per pound. You can cut larger shrimp into small pieces instead of buying small shrimp if you'd like.

Nutrition: Calories: 198; Total fat: 10g; Saturated fat: 4g; Sodium: 238mg; Phosphorus: 260mg; Potassium: 261mg; Carbohydrates: 9g; Fiber: 1g; Protein: 20g; Sugar: 2g

7. Ginger-Mango Tuna Pasta Salad

Preparation Time: 20 minutes

Cooking Time: 9 minutes

Servings: 6

Ingredients:

- 3 cups whole-wheat ziti pasta
- 1 large navel mango, zested and juiced
- ¼ cup extra-virgin olive oil
- 2 tablespoons yellow prepared mustard
- ¼ teaspoon ground ginger
- Pinch salt
- 1 large navel mango, peeled and segmented
- 1 (6-ounce) can light low-sodium tuna, drained

Directions:

1. Bring a large pot of water to a boil. Add the pasta and cook according to package directions, until the pasta is al dente. Drain and set aside.
2. In a large bowl, whisk the mango juice and zest, olive oil, mustard, ginger, and salt until combined. Add the mango segments and tuna and stir to coat.
3. When the pasta is done, drain and add to the bowl with the dressing and other ingredients. Toss to coat.
4. Cover and chill the salad for 2 to 3 hours, stirring once.
5. Increase Protein Tip: To make this a medium-protein recipe, add one more can of drained tuna. The protein content will increase to 19g per serving.

Nutrition: Calories: 305; Total fat: 11g; Saturated fat: 2g; Sodium: 105mg; Phosphorus: 218mg; Potassium: 379mg; Carbohydrates: 43g; Fiber: 6g; Protein: 13g; Sugar: 7g

8. Pineapple-Soy Salmon Stir-Fry

Preparation Time: 15 minutes

Cooking Time: 15 minutes

Servings: 4

Ingredients:

- 1 (8-ounce) can crushed pineapple, strained, reserving juice
- 2 tablespoons low-sodium soy sauce
- 1 tablespoon cornstarch
- 1/8 teaspoon freshly ground black pepper
- 2 tablespoons extra-virgin olive oil
- 2 (6-ounce) salmon fillets without skin, cubed
- 1 (16-ounce) bag frozen stir-fry vegetables

Directions:

1. In a small bowl, whisk the reserved pineapple juice, soy sauce, cornstarch, and pepper and set aside.
2. In a large wok or skillet, heat the olive oil. Add the salmon cubes and stir-fry for 3 to 4 minutes, or until the salmon flakes with a fork. Using a slotted spoon, transfer the salmon to a plate and set aside.
3. Add the frozen vegetables to the wok and stir-fry for another 3 to 4 minutes, or until the vegetables are hot and tender.
4. Return the salmon to the wok and add the pineapple.
5. Whisk the sauce again and add to the wok; stir-fry for 3 to 4 minutes or until the sauce bubbles and has thickened. Serve.
6. Ingredient Tip: You can make this recipe with just about any protein, such as cubed boneless skinless chicken breasts, cod or sole, or peeled and deveined shrimp. To make this recipe gluten-free, use low-sodium tamari instead of soy sauce.

Nutrition: Calories: 280; Total fat: 13g; Saturated fat: 2g; Sodium: 361mg; Phosphorus: 271mg; Potassium: 599mg; Carbohydrates: 21g; Fiber: 3g; Protein: 22g; Sugar: 11g

DINNER

9. Chicken Veronique

Preparation Time: 10 minutes

Cooking Time: 10 minutes

Servings: 4

Ingredients:

- 2 boneless skinless chicken breasts
- 1/2 shallot, chopped
- 2 tablespoons butter
- 2 tablespoons dry white wine
- 2 tablespoons chicken broth
- 1/2 cup green grapes, halved
- 1 teaspoon dried tarragon
- 1/4 cup cream

Directions:

1. Place an 8-inch skillet over medium heat and add butter to melt.
2. Sear the chicken in the melted butter until golden-brown on both sides.
3. Place the boneless chicken on a plate and set it aside.
4. Add shallot to the same skillet and stir until soft.
5. Whisk cornstarch with broth and wine in a small bowl.
6. Pour this slurry into the skillet and mix well.
7. Place the chicken in the skillet and cook it on a simmer for 6 minutes.
8. Transfer the chicken to the serving plate.
9. Add cream, tarragon, and grapes.

10. Cook for 1 minute, and then pour this sauce over the chicken.
11. Serve.

Nutrition: Calories: 306 kcal Total Fat: 18 g Saturated Fat: 0 g Cholesterol: 124 mg Sodium: 167 mg Total Carbs: 9 g

10.   Marinated Shrimp and Pasta

Preparation Time: 10 minutes

Cooking Time: 20 minutes

Servings: 10

Ingredients:

- 12 oz. of three-colored penne pasta
- ½ pound of cooked shrimp
- ½ red bell pepper, diced
- ½ cup of red onion, chopped
- 3 stalks of celery
- 12 baby carrots, cut into thick slices
- 1 cup of cauliflower, cut into small round pieces
- ¼ cup of honey
- ¼ cup balsamic vinegar
- ½ tsp. of black pepper
- ½ tsp. garlic powder
- 1 tbsp. of French mustard
- ¾ cup of olive oil

Directions:

1. Cook pasta for around 10 minutes (or according to packaged instructions).
2. While pasta is boiling, cut all your veggies and place into a large mixing bowl. Add the cooked shrimp.

3. In a mixing bowl, add the honey, vinegar, black pepper, garlic powder, and mustard. While you whisk, slowly incorporate the oil and stir well.
4. Add in the drained pasta with the veggies and shrimp and gently combine everything. Pour the liquid marinade over the pasta and veggies and toss to coat everything evenly.
5. Refrigerate for 3-5 hours before serving. Serve chilled.

Nutrition: Calories: 256kcal Carbohydrate: 41g Protein: 6.55g Sodium: 242.04mg Potassium: 131.88mg Phosphorus: 86.03mg Dietary Fiber: 2.28g Fat: 16.88g

11. Exotic Palabok

Preparation Time: 25 minutes

Cooking Time: 15 minutes

Servings: 6

Ingredients:

- 12 oz. rice noodles.
- 1 ½ cups of medium shrimp, peeled and deveined
- 2/3 cup of white onion, chopped
- 1 spring onion, sliced
- 3 tbsp. of canola oil
- 1-pound, lean ground turkey
- 2 cups of firm tofu, chopped
- 2 packs of shrimp or ordinary gravy mix
- 5 hard-boiled eggs
- 1 lemon
- ½ cup of pork rinds (optional)

Directions:

1. Boil rice noodles until nice and soft. Keep aside.

2. Boil the peeled shrimp for 2-3 minutes in a pot with plain water.
3. In a wok or shallow pan, saute the garlic and onion with the oil. Add the ground turkey, tofu, and shrimps.
4. Dissolve the gravy mix in water or as per package instructions.
5. Combine the rice noodles, tofu, onions, and the gravy mix with ½ cup of pork rind (optional).
6. Slice the egg and lemons.
7. Serve with egg and lemons on top.

Nutrition: Calories: 305 kcal Carbohydrate: 39.14g Protein: 17.6g Sodium: 536mg Potassium: 243.52 mg Phosphorus: 180.41mg Dietary Fiber: 0.9g

MAIN DISHES

12.   Savory Bread

Preparation Time: 10 minutes

Cooking Time: 20-25 minutes

Servings: 8-10

Ingredients:

- ½ cup plus 1tablespoon almond flour
- 1 tsp. baking soda
- 1 teaspoon ground turmeric
- Salt, to taste
- 2 large organic eggs
- 2 organic egg whites
- 1 cup raw cashew butter
- 1 tablespoon water
- 1 tablespoon apple cider vinegar

Directions:

1. Set the oven to 350F. Grease a loaf pan.
2. In a big pan, mix together flour, baking soda, turmeric, and salt.
3. In another bowl, add eggs, egg whites, and cashew butter and beat till smooth.
4. Gradually, add water and beat till well combined.
5. Add flour mixture and mix till well combined.
6. Stir in apple cider vinegar treatment.
7. Place a combination into prepared loaf pan evenly.

8. Bake for around twenty minutes or till a toothpick inserted within the center is released clean.

Nutrition: Calories: 347   Fat: 11g   Carbohydrates: 29g Fiber: 6g Protein: 21g

13.   Savory Veggie Muffins

Preparation Time: 15 minutes

Cooking Time: 18-23 minutes

Servings: 5

Ingredients:

- ¾ cup almond meal
- ½ tsp baking soda
- ¼ cup concentrate powder
- 2 teaspoons fresh dill, chopped
- Salt, to taste
- 4 large organic eggs
- 1½ tablespoons nutritional yeast
- 2 teaspoons apple cider vinegar
- 3 tablespoons fresh lemon juice
- 2 tablespoons coconut oil, melted
- 1 cup coconut butter, softened
- 1 bunch scallion, chopped
- 2 medium carrots, peeled and grated
- ½ cup fresh parsley, chopped

Directions:

1. Set the oven to 350F. Grease 10 cups of your large muffin tin.
2. In a large bowl, mix together flour, baking soda, Protein powder, and salt.

3. In another bowl, add eggs, nutritional yeast, vinegar, lemon juice, and oil and beat till well combined.
4. Add coconut butter and beat till the mixture becomes smooth.
5. Put egg mixture into the flour mixture and mix till well combined.
6. Fold in scallion, carts, and parsley.
7. Place the amalgamation into prepared muffin cups evenly.
8. Bake for about 18-23 minutes or till a toothpick inserted inside center comes out clean.

Nutrition: Calories: 378 Fat: 13g Carbohydrates: 32g Fiber: 11g Protein: 32g

14. Crepes with Coconut Cream & Strawberry Sauce

Preparation Time: 15 minutes

Cooking Time: 8 minutes

Servings: 4

Ingredients:

- For Sauce:
- 12-ounces frozen strawberries, thawed and liquid reserved
- 1½ teaspoons tapioca starch
- 1 tablespoon honey
- For the Coconut cream:
- 1 (13½-ounce) can chilled coconut almond milk
- 1 teaspoon organic vanilla flavoring
- 1 tablespoon organic honey
- For Crepes:

- 2 tablespoons tapioca starch
- 2 tablespoons coconut flour
- ¼ cup almond milk
- 2 organic eggs
- Pinch of salt
- Almond oil, as required

Directions:

1. For sauce inside a bowl, mix together some reserved strawberry liquid and tapioca starch.
2. Add remaining ingredients and mix well.
3. Transfer a combination inside a pan on medium-high heat.
4. Bring to a boil, stirring continuously.
5. Cook for at least 2-3 minutes, till the sauce, becomes thick.
6. Remove from heat and aside, covered till serving.
7. For coconut cream, carefully, scoop your cream from your surface of a can of coconut almond milk.
8. In a mixer, add coconut cream, vanilla flavoring, and honey and pulse for around 6-8 minutes or till fluffy.
9. For crepes in a blender, add all ingredients and pulse till well combined and smooth.
10. Lightly, grease a substantial nonstick skillet with almond oil as well as heat on medium-low heat.
11. Add a modest amount of mixture and tilt the pan to spread it evenly inside the skillet.
12. Cook approximately 1-2 minutes.
13. Carefully change the side and cook for approximately 1-1½ minutes more.
14. Repeat with the remaining mixture.
15. Divide the coconut cream onto each crepe evenly and fold into quarters.

16. Place strawberry sauce ahead and serve.
Nutrition: Calories: 364 Fat: 9g Carbohydrates: 26g Fiber: 7g Protein: 15g

SNACKS

15. Grilled Peppers in Chipotle Vinaigrette

Preparation Time: 15 minutes

Cooking Time: 6 minutes

Serving: 4

Ingredients:

- 1 red bell pepper
- 1 yellow bell pepper
- 1 mango bell pepper
- 2 tablespoons extra-virgin olive oil
- Juice of 1 lemon
- 1 tsp. minced chipotle peppers in adobo sauce

Direction

1. Prepare and preheat the grill to medium coals and set a grill 6 inches from the coals. If grilling indoors, heat the grill pan over medium-high heat. For charcoal grills, medium coals mean you can hold your palm 6 inches above the grill rack for 3 to 4 seconds before you have to take it away. For gas and propane grills, medium coals are 350°F to 375°F.
2. Wash the bell peppers, remove the seeds, and cut them into 1-inch strips.
3. Blend olive oil, lemon juice, and chipotle peppers in adobo sauce.
4. Place the peppers on the grill and brush with some of the sauce. Grill the peppers for 2 to 3 minutes per side,

brushing with the sauce occasionally, until the vegetables are tender and have defined grill marks. Serve.

Nutrition: 66 Calories 90mg Sodium 22mg Phosphorus 201mg Potassium 1g Protein

16.   Hummus Deviled Eggs

Preparation Time: 10 minutes

Cooking Time: 0 minutes

Servings: 6

Ingredients:

- 6 hard-boiled eggs
- 1/2 cup hummus
- Paprika

Directions:

1. Slice the hardboiled eggs in half lengthwise and remove the yolk.
2. Fill the egg whites with hummus and sprinkle with paprika before serving.

Nutrition: Calories: 179 kcal Protein: 11.03 g Fat: 12.41 g Carbohydrates: 5.14 g

17.Hummus with Celery

Preparation Time: 15 minutes

Cooking Time: 0 minutes

Servings: 4

Ingredients:

- 1/4 cup lemon juice

- 1/4 cup tahini
- 3 cloves of garlic, crushed
- 2 tablespoons extra virgin olive oil
- 1/2 teaspoon salt
- 1/2 teaspoon cumin
- 1 (15–ounce) can chickpeas
- 2 to 3 tablespoons water
- Dash of paprika
- 6 stalks celery, cut into 2-inch pieces
- 3 tablespoons salsa

Directions:

1. Using a food processor mix the lemon juice and tahini for about a minute, until it is smooth. Scrape the sides down and process for 30 more seconds.
2. Add the garlic, olive oil, salt, and cumin. Blend for about 1 minute.
3. Drain the chickpeas, put the half of them on the food processor, and blend for another minute. Scrape down the sides, add the other half of the chickpeas, and process until smooth, about 2 minutes. If it like a little too thick, add water, 1 tablespoon at a time until you reach the desired consistency.
4. Fill the celery sticks with hummus and sprinkle paprika on top.
5. Serve with salsa for dipping.

Nutrition: Calories: 240 kcal Protein: 9.27 g Fat: 14.51 g Carbohydrates: 21.01 g

18.   Lemony Ginger Cookies

Preparation Time: 15 minutes + 30 minutes chill time

Cooking Time: 10-12 minutes

Servings: 25

Ingredients:

- 1/2 cup arrowroot flour
- 1 1/2 cups stevia
- 3/4 teaspoon salt
- 1/2 teaspoon baking soda
- 1 teaspoon nutritional yeast
- 3 inches of ginger root, peeled and diced
- 1 1/2 cup coconut butter, softened
- Zest of 1 lemon
- 2 teaspoons vanilla

Directions:

1. Set the oven to 350F, then line two or three cookie sheets with parchment paper.
2. Mix the arrowroot flour, stevia, salt, soda, and yeast in a bowl.
3. In another bowl, put the remaining ingredients and mix well.
4. Put in the dry ingredients gradually until well combined. If the dough is too soft, put an additional 1 to 2 tablespoons of arrowroot powder. The dough will stiffen when chilled, so be careful.
5. Wrap the dough in parchment and press it flat. Chill for 30 minutes.
6. Take a chunk of the chilled dough and flatten it between two pieces of parchment until it is 1/8 inch thick. Dust with a little arrowroot powder and cut into shapes.

7. Place on baking sheets about 1 inch apart and bake 10 to 12 minutes. Cool on cookie sheets for 15 minutes before removing.

Nutrition: Calories: 112 kcal Protein: 0.44 g Fat: 11.3 g Carbohydrates: 2.49 g

SOUP AND STEW

19.   Quick Pea Soup

Preparation Time: 5 mins

Cooking time 15 mins

Serving 3

Ingredients:

- 300 g Carrots
- 1 onion
- 1 toe garlic
- 30 g butter
- 200 g cream
- 1 Bay leaf
- 400 g frozen peas
- Salt
- Pepper
- Nutmeg
- Cumin
- As required: smoked salmon

Direction:

1. Peel the carrots, onion, and garlic and cut into cubes.
2. Melt the butter and sauté carrots, onions, and garlic in it.
3. Deglaze with cream, fill the cup twice with water and add this as well. Season with salt, pepper, freshly grated nutmeg, and cumin.

4. Add the bay leaf and cook everything until the carrots are done. Take out the bay leaf and add the peas.
5. Bring to the boil again and then puree with a hand blender. If the soup is still too thick, add 1 more shot of water.
6. Season again to taste and serve. Add smoked salmon strips to the soup to taste.

Nutritional values: Calories/Energy: 61 Kcal, Protein: 3.2 g Carbs: 9.88 g Calcium: 12 mg, Phosphorous: 47 mg, Potassium: 71 mg, Sodium: 336 mg

20.   Chickpea Soup with Croutons

Preparation time 20 mins

Cooking time 45 mins

Serving: 1 – 4

Ingredients:

- Dried chickpeas 60 g
- Common bread without salt 80 g
- Extra virgin olive oil 20 g
- Rosemary
- Sage
- Garlic
- Bay leaf
- Chili

Direction:

1. Soak the chickpeas the night before.
2. Bring to a boil to pots of water.
3. Meanwhile, prepare a sauté with chopped rosemary, a bit of garlic, oil, sage, a few bay leaves, and a little chili. When the garlic is golden, it should be removed.

4. Pour the chickpeas into boiling water, drain them after a quarter of an hour and dip them back into the second pot of boiling water. Leave to cook for another quarter of an hour.

5. Add some chickpeas to the mixture and place them in a small pan with some of their water. The others must be blended to create a cream that we can make more or less thick with your water. Add the whole chickpeas, bring to the boil again and add the common pasta.

6. Serve accompanied with common wood baked toasted bread, adding a drizzle of extra virgin olive oil.

Nutrition: Protein: 23 g, Phosphorous: 241mg, Potassium: 609 mg, Carbs: 81 g, Sodium: 8 mg, Calories: 594 kcal

21. Tomato Soup Made from Fresh Red bell peppers

Preparation Time: 20mins

Cooking Time: 20mins

Servings 2

Ingredients:

- 1 kg of Red bell peppers
- 200 ml of water
- ½ teaspoon salt
- 1 sprig of rosemary
- 1 sprig of thyme
- 2 tbsp. cream
- 2 tbsp. sour cream

Direction:

1. Wash the Red bell peppers and put them in a saucepan with water and salt. Bring to a boil. Simmer for until the peel starts to peel off the Red bell peppers and the Red bell peppers are soft.
2. In the meantime, wash the herbs and let them dry on kitchen paper.
3. Drain the Red bell peppers, collecting the cooking water if necessary. Strain or strain the soft Red bell peppers through a sieve. Let the pureed Red bell peppers simmer for about 10 minutes. Then stir with the cream until smooth. Dilute with some of the collected cooking water as desired.
4. Strip off the rosemary and thyme needles and chop finely. Pour the soup into two bowls, put a dollop of sour cream on top and sprinkle everything with the herbs.

Nutrition: Calories186 kcal, Protein 6g Fat 8 g Carbohydrates 21g

22.   Chicken Noodle Soup

Preparation Time: 10 minutes

Cooking Time: 25 minutes

Servings: 2

Ingredients:

- 1 1/2 cups low-sodium vegetable broth
- 1 cup of water
- 1/4 tsp poultry seasoning
- 1/4 tsp black pepper
- 1 cup chicken strips
- 1/4 cup carrot
- 2 oz. egg noodles, uncooked

Direction:

1. Cook soup on high heat for 25 minutes in a slow cooker.
2. Serve warm.

Nutrition: Calories 103. Protein 8 g. Carbohydrates 11 g. Fat 3 g. Cholesterol 4 mg. Sodium 355 mg.

Potassium 264 mg. Phosphorus 128 mg. Calcium 46 mg. Fiber 4.0 g.

VEGETABLE

23.   Vegetarian Taco Salad

Preparation Time: 15 minutes

Cooking Time: 15 minutes

Servings: 2

Ingredients:

- 1½ cups canned low-sodium or no-salt-added pinto beans, rinsed and drained
- 1 (10-ounce) package frozen white rice, thawed
- 1 red bell pepper, chopped
- 3 scallions, white and green parts, chopped
- 1 jalapeño pepper, minced
- 1 cup frozen corn, thawed and drained
- 1 tablespoon chili powder
- 1 cup chopped romaine lettuce
- 2 cups chopped butter lettuce
- ½ cup Powerhouse Salsa
- ½ cup grated pepper Jack cheese

Directions:

1. In a medium bowl, combine the beans, rice, bell pepper, scallions, jalapeño, and corn.
2. Sprinkle with the chili powder and stir gently.
3. Stir in the romaine and butter lettuce.
4. Serve topped with Powerhouse Salsa and cheese.

Nutrition: Calories: 254 Fat: 7g Carbohydrates: 39g Protein: 11g Sodium: 440mg Potassium: 599mg Phosphorus: 240mg

24.   Double-Boiled Country Style Fried Carrots

Preparation Time: 20 minutes

Cooking Time: 20 minutes

Servings: 4

Ingredients:

- ½ cup canola oil
- ¼ tsp ground cumin
- ¼ tsp paprika
- ¼ tsp white pepper
- 3 tbsp. ketchup

Directions:

1. Soak or double boil the carrots if you are on a low potassium diet.
2. Heat oil over medium heat in a skillet.
3. Fry the carrots for around 10 minutes until golden brown.
4. Drain carrots, then sprinkle with cumin, pepper, and paprika.
5. Serve with ketchup or mayo.

Nutrition: Calories 156 Fat 0.1g Carbs 21g Protein 2gSodium 3mg Potassium 296mg Phosphorous 34mg

25.   Double-Boiled Stewed Carrots

Preparation Time: 20 minutes

Cooking Time: 30 minutes

Servings: 4

Ingredients:

- 2 cup carrots, diced into ½ inch cubes
- ½ cup hot water
- ½ cup liquid non-dairy creamer
- ¼ tsp garlic powder
- ¼ tsp black pepper
- 2 tbsp. margarine
- 2 tsp all-purpose white flour

Directions:

1. Soak or double boil the carrots if you are on a low potassium diet.
2. Boil carrots for 15 minutes.
3. Drain carrots and return to pan. Add half a cup of hot water, the creamer, garlic powder, pepper, and margarine. Heat to a boil.
4. Mix the flour with a tablespoon of water and then stir this into the carrots. Cook for 3 minutes until the mixture has thickened and the flour has cooked.

Nutrition: Calories 184 Carbs 25g Protein 2g Potassium 161mg Phosphorous 65mg

SIDE DISHES

26.   Squash and Cranberries

Preparation Time: 10 minutes

Cooking Time: 30 minutes

Servings: 2

Ingredients:

- 1 tablespoon coconut oil
- 1 butternut squash, peeled and cubed
- 2 garlic cloves, minced
- 1 small yellow onion, chopped
- 12 ounces coconut almond milk
- 1 teaspoon curry powder
- 1 teaspoon cinnamon powder
- ½ cup cranberries

Directions:

1. Spread squash pieces on a lined baking sheet, place in the oven at 425 degrees F, bake for 15 minutes and leave to one side.
2. Heat up a pan with the oil over medium high heat, add garlic and onion, stir and cook for 5 minutes.
3. Add roasted squash, stir and cook for 3 minutes.
4. Add coconut almond milk, cranberries, cinnamon and curry powder, stir and cook for 5 minutes more.
5. Divide between plates and serve as a side dish!
6. Enjoy!

Nutrition: Calories 518, fat 47, 6, fiber 7, 3, carbs 24, 9, protein 5, 3 Phosphorus: 110mg Potassium: 117mg Sodium: 75mg

SALAD

27.   Healthy Cucumber Salad

Preparation Time: 10 minutes

Cooking Time: 5 minutes

Servings: 4

Ingredients:

- 2 cucumbers, cubed
- 2 tbsp. fresh lime juice
- 1 tbsp. lemon juice
- 2 tbsp. green onion, minced
- 1 garlic, minced
- 1/4 cup fresh cilantro, chopped
- Pepper
- Salt

Directions:

1. In a small bowl, whisk together lime juice, lemon juice, garlic, pepper, and salt.
2. Add cucumber, green onion, cilantro, into the medium bowl and mix well.
3. Pour dressing over salad and mix.
4. Cover and place in the refrigerator for 30 minutes.
5. Serve chilled and enjoy.

Nutrition: Calories 239 Fat 19.8 g Carbohydrates 17.1 g Sugar 3.6 g Protein 3.2 g Cholesterol 0 mg Phosphorus: 130mg Potassium: 127mg Sodium: 75mg

28.   Egg Tuna Salad

Preparation Time: 10 minutes

Cooking Time: 5 minutes

Servings: 6

Ingredients:

- 8 eggs, hard-boiled, peeled and chopped
- 1/8 tsp paprika
- 1 tsp Dijon mustard
- 2 tbsp. mayonnaise
- 1/3 cup yogurt
- 2 tbsp. chives, minced
- 2 tbsp. onion, minced
- 5 oz. tuna, drain
- Pepper
- Salt

Directions:

1. In a large bowl, whisk together mustard, mayonnaise, yogurt, pepper, and salt.
2. Add eggs, chives, onion, and tuna and mix well.
3. Sprinkle with paprika and serve.

Nutrition: Calories 159 Fat 9.6 g Carbohydrates 3 g Sugar 1.9 g Protein 14.6 g Cholesterol 228 mg Phosphorus: 110mg Potassium: 117mg Sodium: 75mg

FISH & SEAFOOD

29.   Lemon-Herb Grilled Fish

Preparation Time: 5 minutes

CookingTime:10minutes
Servings: 4

Ingredients:

- 4 peeled garlic cloves
- ¼ tsp. salt
- 8 lemon slices
- ¼ tsp. ground black pepper
- Remoulade
- 2 small blue-fish
- 2 sprigs fresh thyme

Directions:

1. Prepare outdoor grill with medium-low to medium coals, or heat gas grill to medium-low to medium (to broil, see Note below).
2. Rinse fish; pat dry. Cut 3 slashes on each side. Season with salt, pepper.
3. Stuff 3 lemon slices in cavity of each fish. Add thyme and 2 cloves garlic to each cavity.
4. Grill fish 6 inches from heat, covered, 10 to 12 minutes, until just beginning to char. flip over carefully. Cover each eye with one of remaining lemon slices. Grill 12 to 15 minutes more, until flesh is white throughout.

5. Transfer fish to platter. For each, pry up top fillet in one piece, flipping over, and skin side down.
6. Beginning at tail, carefully pull up end of spine of fish, and lift up, removing whole backbone. Remove any small bones from fish.
7. Serve with Remoulade.

Nutrition: Calories: 118.1, Fat: 6.8 g, Carbs: 1 g, Protein: 12.9 g, Sugars: 12.9 g, Sodium: 91.2 mg

30. Cod Peas

Preparation Time: 18-20 minutes

CookingTime:40minutes
Servings: 4-5

Ingredients:

- 1 c. peas
- 2 tbsps. Capers
- 4 de-boned medium cod fillets
- 3 tbsps. Olive oil
- ¼ tsp. black pepper
- 2 tbsps. Lime juice
- 2 tbsps. Chopped shallots
- 1 ½ tbsps. Chopped oregano

Directions:

1. Heat up 1 tbsp. olive oil in a saucepan over medium flame
2. Add the fillets, cook for 5 minutes on each side; set aside.
3. In a bowl of large size, thoroughly mix the oregano, shallots, lime juice, peas, capers, black pepper, and 2 tbsp. olive oil.

4. Toss and serve with the cooked fish.

Nutrition: Calories: 224, Fat: 11 g, Carbs: 7 g, Protein: 24 g, Sugars: 2 g, Sodium: 485 mg

31.   Baked Haddock

Preparation Time: 10 minutes

CookingTime:10minutes
Servings: 4

Ingredients:

- 1 tsp. chopped dill
- 3 tsps. Water
- ¼ tsp. black pepper and salt
- Cooking spray
- 1 lb. chopped haddock
- 2 tbsps. Fresh lemon juice

Directions:

1. Spray a baking dish with a few oils, add fish, water, freshly squeezed lemon juice, salt, black pepper, mayo and dill, toss, introduce inside the oven and bake at 350 0F for the half-hour.
2. Divide between plates and serve.
3. Enjoy!

Nutrition: Calories: 264, Fat: 4 g, Carbs: 7 g, Protein: 12 g, Sugars: 0 g, Sodium: 71.4 mg

32.   Simple Soup

PreparationTime:05min
CookingTime:15minutes
Servings: 4

Ingredients:

- 2 teaspoons tuna
- 4 cups water
- 1 (8 ounce) package silken tofu, diced
- 2 green onions, sliced diagonally into 1/2-inch pieces

Directions:

1. In a medium saucepan over medium-high heat, combine tuna and water; bring to a boil.
2. Reduce heat to medium, Stir in tofu.
3. Separate the layers of the green onions, and add them to the soup.
4. Simmer gently for 2 to 3 minutes before serving.

Nutrition: Calories 77, Total Fat 3.3g, Saturated Fat 0.6g, Cholesterol 7mg, Sodium 39mg, Total Carbohydrate 1.9g, Dietary Fiber 0.3g, Total Sugars 0.9g, Protein 9.7g, Calcium 32mg, Iron 1mg, Potassium 104mg, Potassium 88mg

33.   Turkey Sloppy Joes

Preparation Time: 15 minutes

Cooking Time: 4 to 6 hours

Servings: 4

Ingredients:

- 1 tablespoon extra-virgin olive oil
- 1 pound ground turkey
- 1 celery stalk, minced
- 1 carrot, minced
- ½ medium sweet onion, diced
- ½ red bell pepper, finely chopped
- 6 tablespoons tomato paste
- 2 tablespoons apple cider vinegar
- 1 tablespoon maple syrup
- 1 teaspoon Dijon mustard
- 1 teaspoon chili powder
- ½ teaspoon garlic powder
- ½ teaspoon sea salt
- ½ teaspoon dried oregano

Directions:

1. In your slow cooker, combine the olive oil, turkey, celery, carrot, onion, red bell pepper, tomato paste, vinegar, maple syrup, mustard, chili powder, garlic powder, salt, and oregano. Using a large spoon, break

up the turkey into smaller chunks as it combines with the other ingredients.

2. Cover the cooker and set to low. Cook for 4 to 6 hours, stir thoroughly and serve.

Nutrition: Calories: 251 Total Fat: 12g Total Carbs: 14g Sugar: 9g Fiber: 3g

Protein: 24g Sodium: 690mg

34.   Balsamic-Glazed Turkey Wings

Preparation Time: 15 minutes

Cooking Time: 7 to 8 hours

Servings: 4

Ingredients:

- 1¼ cups balsamic vinegar
- 2 tablespoons raw honey
- 1 teaspoon garlic powder
- 2 pounds turkey wings

Directions:

1. In a bowl, put together the vinegar, honey, and garlic powder then mix.
2. Put the wings in the bottom of the slow cooker, and pour the vinegar sauce on top.
3. Cover the cooker and set to low. Cook for 7 to 8 hours.
4. Baste the wings with the sauce from the bottom of the slow cooker and serve.

Nutrition: Calories: 501 Total Fat: 25g Sugar: 9g Fiber: 0g Protein: 47g Sodium: 162mg

35.   Smokey Turkey Chili

Preparation Time: 5 Minutes

Cooking Time: 45 Minutes

Servings: 8

Ingredients:

- 12-ounce lean ground turkey
- 1/2 red onion, chopped
- 2 cloves garlic, crushed and chopped
- 1/2 teaspoon of smoked paprika
- 1/2 teaspoon of chili powder
- 1/2 teaspoon of dried thyme
- 1/4 cup reduced-sodium beef stock
- 1/2 cup of water
- 11/2 cups baby green lettuce leaves, washed
- 3 wheat tortillas

Directions:

1. Brown the ground beef in a dry skillet over medium-high heat.
2. Add in the red onion and garlic.
3. Sauté the onion until it goes clear.
4. Transfer the contents of the skillet to the slow cooker.
5. Add the remaining ingredients and simmer on low for 30–45 minutes.
6. Stir through the green lettuce for the last few minutes to wilt.
7. Slice tortillas and gently toast under the broiler until slightly crispy.
8. Serve on top of the turkey chili.

Nutrition: Calories 93.5, Protein 8g, Carbohydrates 3g, Fat 5.5g, Cholesterol 30.5mg, Sodium 84.5mg, Potassium 142.5mg, Phosphorus 92.5mg, Calcium 29mg, Fiber 0.5g

MEAT RECIPES

36.   Stir-Fried Ground Beef

Preparation Time: 10 minutes

Cooking Time: 15 minutes

Servings: 4

Ingredients:

- 1/2 cup broccoli, chopped
- 1/2 of medium-sized onions, chopped
- 1/2 of medium-sized red bell pepper, chopped
- 1 tbsp. cayenne pepper (optional)
- 1 tbsp. Chinese five spices
- 1 tbsp. coconut oil
- 1-lb ground beef
- 2 kale leaves, chopped
- 5 medium-sized mushrooms, sliced

Directions:

1. In a skillet, heat the coconut oil over medium high heat.
2. Sauté the onions for one minute and add the vegetables while stirring constantly.
3. Add the ground beef and the spices.
4. Cook for two minutes and reduce the heat to medium.
5. Cover the skillet and continue to cook the beef and vegetables for another 10 minutes.
6. Serve and enjoy.

Nutrition: Calories 304, Total Fat 17g, Saturated Fat 3g, Total Carbs 6g, Net Carbs 4g, Protein 32g, Sugar: 2g, Fiber 2g, Sodium 86mg, Potassium 624mg

37.   Lamb with Zucchini & Couscous

Preparation Time: 15 minutes

Cooking Time: 8 minutes

Servings: 2

Ingredients:

- ¾ cup couscous
- ¾ cup boiling water
- 1/4 cup fresh cilantro, chopped
- 1 tbsp. olive oil
- 5-ounces lamb leg steak, cubed into ¾-inch size
- 1 medium zucchini, sliced thinly
- 1 medium red onion, cut into wedges
- 1 teaspoon ground cumin
- 1 teaspoon ground coriander
- 1/4 teaspoon red pepper flakes, crushed
- Salt, to taste
- 1/4 cup plain Greek yogurt
- 1 garlic herb, minced

Directions:

1. In a bowl, add couscous and boiling water and stir to combine,
2. Cover whilst aside approximately 5 minutes.
3. Add cilantro and with a fork, fluff completely.
4. Meanwhile in a substantial skillet, heat oil on high heat.

5. Add lamb and stir fry for about 2-3 minutes.
6. Add zucchini and onion and stir fry for about 2 minutes.
7. Stir in spices and stir fry for about 1 minute
8. Add couscous and stir fry approximately 2 minutes.
9. In a bowl, mix together yogurt and garlic.
10. Divide lamb mixture in serving plates evenly.
11. Serve using the topping of yogurt.

Nutrition: Calories: 392, Fat: 5g, Carbohydrates: 2g, Fiber: 12g, Protein: 35g

BROTHS, CONDIMENT AND SEASONING

38.   Tex-Mex Seasoning Mix

Preparation Time: 10 minutes

Cooking Time: 0 minutes

Servings: 2 tbsp.

Ingredients:

- 1 tablespoon chili powder
- ½ teaspoon ground cumin
- ½ teaspoon dried oregano leaves
- ½ teaspoon garlic powder
- ½ teaspoon onion powder
- ½ teaspoon cayenne pepper
- ½ teaspoon red pepper flakes

Directions:

1. Combine the chili powder, cumin, oregano, garlic powder, onion powder, cayenne pepper, and red pepper flakes. Store for up to 6 months.

Nutrition: Calories: 7 Fat: 0g Sodium: 39mg Potassium: 38mg Phosphorus: 7mg Carbohydrates: 1g Protein: 0g

39.   Everyday No-Salt Seasoning Blend

Preparation Time: 15 minutes

Cooking Time: 0 minutes

Servings: 2 tbsp.

Ingredients:

- 1 teaspoon dried thyme leaves
- 1 teaspoon dried marjoram leaves
- 1 teaspoon dried basil leaves
- 1 teaspoon dried oregano leaves
- ½ teaspoon onion powder
- ½ teaspoon garlic powder

- ½ teaspoon ground mustard
- ¼ teaspoon freshly ground black pepper
- ¼ teaspoon paprika

Directions:

1. Combine the thyme, marjoram, basil, oregano, onion powder, garlic powder, ground mustard, pepper, and paprika. Transfer and store at room temperature for up to 6 months.

Nutrition: Calories: 4 Fat: 0g Sodium: 0mg Potassium: 17mg Phosphorus: 4mg Carbohydrates: 1g Protein: 0g

DESSERT

40.   Dessert cocktail

Preparation time: 1 minutes

Cooking time: 0 minute

Servings: 4

Ingredients:

- 1 cup of cranberry juice
- 1 cup of fresh ripe strawberries, washed and hull removed
- 2 tablespoon of lime juice
- ¼ cup of white sugar
- 8 ice cubes

Directions:

1. Combine all the ingredients in a blender until smooth and creamy.
2. Pour the liquid into chilled tall glasses and serve cold.

Nutrition: Calories: 92 kcal Carbohydrate: 23.5 g Protein: 0.5 g Sodium: 3.62 mg Potassium: 103.78 mg Phosphorus: 17.86 mg Dietary fiber: 0.84 g Fat: 0.17 g

41.   Gingerbread loaf

Preparation time: 20 minutes

Cooking time: 1 hour

Servings: 16

Ingredients:

- Unsalted butter, for greasing the baking dish
- 3 cups all-purpose flour

- ½ teaspoon ener-g baking soda substitute
- 2 teaspoons ground cinnamon
- 1 teaspoon ground allspice
- ¾ cup granulated sugar
- 1¼ cups plain rice almond milk
- 1 large egg
- ¼ cup olive oil
- 2 tablespoons molasses
- 2 teaspoons grated fresh ginger
- Powdered sugar, for dusting

Directions:

1. Preheat the oven to 350°f.
2. Lightly grease a 9-by-13-inch baking dish with butter; set aside.
3. In a large bowl, sift together the flour, baking soda substitute, cinnamon, and allspice.
4. Stir the sugar into the flour mixture.
5. In medium bowl, whisk together the almond milk, egg, olive oil, molasses, and ginger until well blended.
6. Make a well in the center of the flour mixture and pour in the wet ingredients.
7. Mix until just combined, taking care not to over mix.
8. Pour the batter into the baking dish and bake for about 1 hour or until a wooden pick inserted in the middle comes out clean.
9. Serve warm with a dusting of powdered sugar.

Nutrition: calories: 232; fat: 5g; carbohydrates: 42g; phosphorus: 54mg; potassium: 104mg; sodium: 18mg; protein: 4g

DRINKS AND SMOOTHIES

42.   Pinna Colada Protein Smoothie

Preparation Time: 5 minutes

Cooking Time: 2 minutes

Servings: 1

Ingredients:

- 1/2 cup unsweetened vanilla almond milk
- 1/2 cup unsweetened coconut milk
- 3/4 cup frozen pineapple chunks
- 1 scoop vanilla protein powder
- 1 tsp raw honey
- 1 tsp vanilla

Directions:

1. Place almond milk, coconut milk, pineapple, vanilla protein powder, honey, and vanilla in a blender.
2. Blend until smooth. Serve immediately.

Nutrition: Calories: 241 Fat: 7g Carbs: 20g Protein: 26g Sodium: 420mg Potassium: 205mg Phosphorus: 10mg

CONCLUSION

The number one reason why patients are urged to stay healthy during the early stages of kidney disease is to avoid dialysis for as long as possible.

Each recipe has been carefully crafted by a team of experts who have the knowledge and experience to make sure you get the most out of every meal. All of the recipes in this cookbook have been carefully adjusted to ensure that they contain low levels of sodium, potassium, and phosphorus. This is important because these foods provide the necessary vitamins and minerals for people with kidney failure.

This can be done by incorporating the right types of nutrients in your diet, all of which are included in the right amount, in the renal diet. Maintaining your activity levels, getting enough sleep, and quitting bad habits, such as smoking and alcohol, will support your journey towards staying healthy and avoiding dialysis.

Even though there is no cure for chronic kidney disease, it is a journey that you can manage. You can sustain your health and continue living your life as normal, with a high quality of life, for much longer than if you don't follow these basic guidelines.

The number one thing to remember on this journey is that you are in complete control of your outcome.

Recipes from this cookbook are simple, delicious, and healthy. You can even use them as an inspiration to experiment and create your renal diet recipes. Bear in mind that the renal diet is a lifestyle, and to get the best results, it's important to follow it regularly and include it in your daily life. And don't worry, you can do it. After all, this book is the best proof that the renal diet is yummy. Meals do not require too much hassle, and that's also amazing. Without treatments, you could die a very painful death. Renal failure can be the consequence of long-haul diabetes, hypertension, unreliable diet, and can stem from other health concerns.

A renal diet is tied in with directing the intake of protein and phosphorus in your eating routine. Restricting your sodium intake is likewise significant. By controlling these two variables you can control the vast majority of the toxins/waste made by your body and thus this enables your kidney to 100% function. If you get this early enough and truly moderate your diets with extraordinary consideration, you could avert all-out renal failure. If you get this early, you can take out the issue completely.